family
favorites

Published by:
TYPHOON MEDIA CORPORATION
801 12th Avenue South, Suite 400
Naples, Fl 34102 USA

Email: sales@typhoonmediacorp.com
Websites: www.chefexpressinternational.com
         www.typhoonmediacorp.com

Family Favorites
© Typhoon Media Corporation

Publisher
Simon St. John Bailey

Editor-in-chief
Elaine S. Evans

Art Director
Aline Talavera

Food Editor
A. Giribaldi

Includes index
ISBN 9781600814570
UPC 615269145142

2010 Edition
Printed in the United States

index

tomatoes stuffed with olives

ingredients

> 1 cup fresh breadcrumbs
> 1/3 cup chopped black olives
> 2 tablespoons grated

Parmesan cheese
> 1 clove garlic, crushed
> 2 tablespoons olive oil
> freshly ground black pepper
> 4 medium tomatoes

method

1. Combine breadcrumbs, olives, cheese, garlic, oil and black pepper to taste in a bowl.
2. Remove tops from tomatoes and reserve, scoop out pulp. Divide olive mixture between tomatoes. Arrange tomatoes and tops, cut side up, in an ovenproof dish.
3. Place under a preheated hot grill for 5 minutes or until filling is crispy. Replace tops, serve.

Serves 4

smoked chicken salad

ingredients

> 1/4 cup white wine vinegar
> 1/4 cup oil
> 1 tablespoon chopped fresh coriander
> freshly ground black

pepper
> 1/2 cup chopped walnuts, toasted
> 1 smoked chicken, flesh cut into strips
> 2 apples, cored and thickly sliced

method

1. Combine vinegar, oil, coriander and black pepper to taste in a large bowl. Add walnuts, chicken and apples, toss well.

2. Arrange salad on a serving plate. Garnish with fresh dill if desired.

Serves 4

irresistible pizza

ingredients

> **8 small pita bread rounds**
> **$1/2$ cup tomato purée**
> **1 onion, sliced**
> **6 oz/185 g salami, chopped**
> **6 button mushrooms, sliced**
> **1 red or green pepper, chopped**
> **1 oz/30 g pitted black olives, sliced**
> **2 tablespoons chopped fresh herbs**
> **8 oz/250 g grated mozzarella cheese**

method

1. Place pita bread rounds on baking trays and spread with tomato purée. Top with onion, salami, mushrooms, red or green pepper, olives, herbs and mozzarella cheese.

2. Bake at 400°F/200°C/Gas 6 for 10-15 minutes or until cheese melts and bases are crisp.

Makes 8

layered ham loaf

ingredients

> **1 loaf wholemeal bread**
> **1 bunch spinach, cooked and squeezed**
> **6 oz/185 g lean ham, thinly sliced**
> **6 oz/185 g Cheddar cheese, thinly sliced**
> **1 red onion, thinly sliced**
> **2 large tomatoes, sliced**
> **3 oz/90 g sun-dried peppers or tomatoes**
> **1 large avocado, stoned, peeled and thinly sliced**
> **3 tablespoons chopped fresh parsley**

method

1. Cut top from loaf and scoop out center leaving a ¾ in/2 cm border. Reserve top of loaf. Reserve crumbs for another use.

2. Line base of loaf with a layer of spinach leaves. Then top with a layer each of ham, cheese, onion, tomatoes, sun-dried peppers or tomatoes, avocado and parsley. Repeat layers to use all ingredients.

3. Replace top of loaf, press down firmly and wrap tightly in plastic food wrap. Weigh down and chill for at least 1 hour.

Serves 6

vegetable ribbons with pasta

ingredients

> **2 large carrots**
> **4 zucchini**
> **2¹/2 cups cream**
> **1 lb/500 g wide ribbon pasta, freshly cooked**
> **8 thin slices prosciutto, cut into thin strips**
> **¹/2 cup fresh Parmesan cheese, grated**
> **freshly ground black pepper**

method

1. Using a vegetable peeler, peel strips from carrots and zucchini. Blanch strips in boiling water for 1 minute, refresh under cold water and drain.

2. In a large frying pan, bring cream to the boil and reduce by a third. Stir in hot pasta, vegetable ribbons, prosciutto, cheese and black pepper to taste, toss well and serve.

Serves 6

pasta with mushroom sauce

ingredients

> 2 teaspoons olive oil
> 4 strips bacon, chopped
> 4 oz/125 g button mushrooms, sliced
> 1 clove garlic, crushed
> 1 cup cream
> freshly ground black pepper

> 1 small head broccoli, broken into flowerets and cooked
> 12 oz/375 g pasta of your choice, freshly cooked
> 3 tablespoons chopped fresh parsley

method

1. Heat oil in a frying pan and cook bacon for

3-4 minutes or until crisp. Stir in mushrooms and garlic and cook for 2-3 minutes.

2. Pour in cream, bring to the boil, stirring frequently, and simmer for 5 minutes or until sauce thickens. Season to taste with black pepper, add broccoli and heat through.

3. Spoon sauce over hot pasta. Sprinkle with parsley and serve.

Serves 4

seafood and tomato pasta

ingredients

> **1 tablespoon olive oil**
> **4 spring onions, chopped**
> **12 oz/375 g assorted seafood, cooked and chopped**
> **14 oz/440 g canned tomatoes, undrained and mashed**
> **1/2 cup dry white wine**
> **1 tablespoon chopped fresh basil**
> **freshly ground black pepper**
> **12 oz/375 g pasta of your choice, freshly cooked**

method

1. Heat oil in a saucepan and cook spring onions for 1 minute. Stir in seafood and cook for 2 minutes longer.

2. Combine tomatoes and wine and pour into pan. Bring to the boil, then reduce heat and simmer, uncovered, for 10 minutes.

3. Add basil and black pepper to taste and spoon sauce over hot pasta.

Serves 4

sweet potato frittata

ingredients

> 1 teaspoon oil
> 2 sweet potatoes, chopped
> 4 strips bacon, chopped
> 6 eggs, lightly beaten
> 1/2 cup milk
> 3 tablespoons chopped fresh chives
> 2 oz/60 g mature Cheddar cheese, grated
> freshly ground black pepper

method

1. Heat oil in a frying pan over medium heat, add sweet potatoes and bacon and cook, stirring, for 5 minutes or until potatoes are soft.

2. Whisk eggs and milk in a bowl until combined. Pour over potato mixture and cook gently for 4 minutes or until frittata is almost set.

3. Sprinkle with chives, cheese and black pepper to taste. Place pan under a preheated hot grill and cook for 1 minute or until top is golden.

Serves 4

eggs florentine

ingredients

> **3 oz/90 g butter**
> **1¹/2 oz/45 g flour**
> **2 cups milk**
> **4 oz/125 g mature Cheddar cheese, grated**
> **freshly ground black pepper**
> **8 oz/250 g frozen chopped spinach, thawed and squeezed**
> **6 eggs**
> **1 oz/30 g grated Parmesan cheese**

method

1. Melt 2 oz/60 g butter in a saucepan over medium heat, stir in flour and cook for 1 minute. Remove from heat and gradually whisk in milk. Return to heat and stir until sauce boils and thickens. Remove from heat, add Cheddar cheese and black pepper to taste and stir until smooth. Cool.

2. Divide spinach between individual ramekins and make a depression in spinach. Break an egg into each depression, spoon sauce over, sprinkle with Parmesan cheese and dot with remaining butter. Bake at 350ºF/180ºC/ Gas 4 for 15-20 minutes or until golden. Serve immediately.

Serves 6

bean enchiladas

ingredients

- **12 oz/375 g dried red kidney beans, cooked**
- **4 oz/125 g canned creamed sweet corn**
- **2 tablespoons sour cream**
- **12 tortillas**
- **2 oz/60 g mature**
- **Cheddar cheese, grated**
- **4 tomatoes, chopped**
- **2 tablespoons sliced stuffed green olives**
- **2 tablespoons chopped fresh coriander**
- **freshly ground black pepper**

method

1. Combine beans, sweet corn and sour cream. Spoon mixture down the center of each tortilla and roll up.

2. Arrange rolls in a lightly greased ovenproof dish, sprinkle with cheese and bake at 350°F/180°C/Gas 4 for 20-25 minutes.

3. Mix tomatoes, olives, coriander and black pepper to taste in a bowl, spoon over rolls and serve.

Serves 6

ricotta and hazelnut potatoes

ingredients

> 4 large potatoes
> 1/2 cup ricotta cheese
> 2 tablespoons grated Parmesan cheese
> 1/4 cup canned asparagus, drained and chopped
> 1 tablespoon chopped fresh chives
> freshly ground black pepper
> 2 tablespoons chopped hazelnuts

method

1. Boil potatoes until just tender, drain. Cut tops off and discard. Carefully scoop out flesh, leaving a thin border.
2. In a small bowl mix together potato flesh, ricotta, Parmesan cheese, asparagus, chives and black pepper to taste.
3. Fill each potato with mixture and top with hazelnuts. Bake at 350°F/180°C/Gas 4 for 20-25 minutes.

Serves 4

fish and crispy chips

ingredients

> 1 cup all purpose flour
> 1 cup beer
> 2 eggs, separated
> 1 tablespoon oil

> freshly ground black pepper
> 2 lb/1 kg potatoes, sliced
> oil for deep frying
> 6 firm white fish fillets

method

1. Sift flour into a bowl and make a well in the center. Pour in combined beer, egg yolks, oil and black pepper to taste and mix to make a smooth batter. Stand for 20 minutes.

2. Soak potatoes in cold water for 10 minutes. Drain and pat dry on paper towels. Heat oil in a large saucepan and cook chips, in batches, for 5 minutes or until soft but not brown. Drain well on paper towels. Just prior to serving, reheat oil and cook chips for 5 minutes or until golden and crisp. Drain on paper towels and keep warm.

3. Beat egg whites until stiff peaks form, fold into batter. Reheat oil, dip fish in batter, drain off excess and cook, in batches, for 4-5 minutes or until crisp and golden. Drain on paper towels. Serve immediately with chips.

Serves 6

fish with italian sauce

ingredients

> 4 firm white fish steaks
> 2 tablespoons lemon juice
> 6 spring onions, chopped
> 1 clove garlic, crushed
> 14 oz/440 g canned tomatoes
> 4 oz/125 g button mushrooms, sliced
> $^1/_2$ cup red wine
> 1 tablespoon chopped fresh basil
> freshly ground black pepper
> 2 tablespoons grated Parmesan cheese

method

1. Brush fish steaks with lemon juice. Place under a preheated medium grill and cook for 4-5 minutes each side. Keep warm.
2. Place spring onions, garlic, tomatoes, mushrooms, wine, basil and black pepper to taste in a saucepan.

Bring to the boil. Reduce heat and simmer
for 8-10 minutes.
3. Arrange fish steaks on serving plates. Spoon sauce
over and top with Parmesan cheese.

Serves 4

trout and new potatoes

ingredients
> **8 sprigs fresh thyme**
> **4 rainbow trout**
> **3 oz/90 g butter**
> **16 new potatoes, cooked**
and halved
> **freshly ground black pepper**
> **2 tablespoons chopped parsley**

method
1. Place 2 thyme sprigs inside each trout. Heat butter
in a large frying pan and cook trout for 5 minutes.
2. Turn trout, add potatoes and cook, turning potatoes
occasionally, for 5 minutes longer or until trout is
cooked through and potatoes are golden.
3. Season to taste with black pepper, place on serving
plates, sprinkle with parsley. Serve immediately.

Serves 4

salmon soufflés

ingredients
> **7 oz/220 g canned red salmon, drained and flaked**
> **3 oz/90 g bottled**
oysters, drained and chopped (optional)
> **1 teaspoon chopped fresh dill**
> **2-3 dashes hot chili sauce**

> **1 cup cottage cheese**
> **freshly ground black**

    pepper
> **4 egg whites**

method

1. Combine salmon, oysters (if using), dill, chili sauce, cottage cheese and black pepper to taste in a bowl.

2. Beat egg whites until stiff peaks form and fold into salmon mixture. Spoon into lightly greased individual soufflé dishes and bake at 400°F/200°C/ Gas 6 for 30-35 minutes.

Serves 4

roasted chicken with carrots

ingredients

> **5 sprigs fresh rosemary**
> **3 lb/1.5 kg whole chicken**
> **5 carrots, halved lengthwise**
> **2 tablespoons honey, warmed**
> **2 tablespoons butter, melted**
> **1 teaspoon ground white pepper**

method

1. Place 3 rosemary sprigs into chicken cavity. Place chicken and carrots in a large baking dish.

2. Melt honey and butter in a small saucepan over medium heat, add white pepper and leaves of remaining rosemary.
3. Brush honey mixture over chicken. Bake at 350°F/180°C/ Gas 4 for 45-50 minutes, basting with honey mixture and turning carrots frequently.

Serves 4

chicken stir-fry

ingredients

> 1 tablespoon oil
> 1 lb/500 g boneless chicken breast fillets, thinly sliced
> 11 oz/350 g broccoli, broken into flowerets
> 2 small zucchini, chopped
> 1 carrot, sliced
> 1 red pepper, sliced
> 2 teaspoons grated fresh ginger
> 3 tablespoons soy sauce
> 2 teaspoons cornstarch blended with 1 tablespoon water

method

1. Heat oil in a nonstick frying pan over medium heat, add chicken and stir-fry for 3-4 minutes or until tender. Remove from pan and set aside.

2. Add broccoli, zucchini, carrot and red pepper to pan and stir-fry for 2-3 minutes. Stir in ginger, soy sauce and cornstarch mixture and cook, stirring, for 2-3 minutes or until sauce boils and thickens.

3. Return chicken to pan and stir-fry for 2-3 minutes or until heated through. Serve on a bed of noodles if desired.

Serves 4

sweet chicken drumsticks

ingredients

> 8 chicken drumsticks
> 3 tablespoons apricot jam, warmed
> 6 oz/185 g all purpose flour
> freshly ground black pepper
> 3 oz/90 g cornmeal
> 2 eggs, beaten
> oil for deep frying

method

1. Brush each drumstick with jam, then roll in 4 oz/125 g flour. Combine remaining flour with black pepper to taste and cornmeal. Dip drumsticks in eggs, then coat with cornmeal mixture.

2. Fry drumsticks in hot oil for 20 minutes until golden and cooked. Drain on paper towels.

Serves 4

quick chicken curry

ingredients

> **2 tablespoons butter**
> **1 onion, chopped**
> **1 clove garlic, crushed**
> **1 green pepper, chopped**
> **3 teaspoons curry paste**
> **1 teaspoon ground cumin**
> **2 tablespoons all purpose flour**
> **2 cups chicken stock**
> **1 cooked chicken, flesh cut into bite-size pieces**

method

1. Melt butter in a large frying pan over medium heat and cook onion, garlic and green pepper for 3-4 minutes or until soft. Add curry paste, cumin and flour and cook for 1 minute longer.

2. Stir in stock and cook, stirring constantly, until mixture boils and thickens. Add chicken and simmer for 3 minutes or until heated through. Serve at once, with rice if desired.

Serves 4

crunchy meatloaf

ingredients

> 1 1/2 lb/750 g ground beef
> 1 potato, grated
> 1 carrot, grated
> 1 onion, finely chopped
> 1/2 cup dried breadcrumbs
> 1 egg, beaten
> 2 tablespoons tomato sauce
> 1 teaspoon dried mixed herbs
> freshly ground black pepper
> 1/2 cup dried breadcrumbs, extra
> 2 oz/60 g butter, melted

method

1. Place beef, potato, carrot, onion, breadcrumbs, egg, tomato sauce, herbs and black pepper to taste in a bowl and mix well to combine.
2. Press mixture into a lightly greased loaf pan and bake at 350ºF/180ºC/Gas 4 for 1 hour or until cooked.
3. Drain off juices and turn meatloaf onto a lightly greased baking tray. Sprinkle with combined breadcrumbs and butter. Bake for 15-20 minutes longer or until topping is crisp and golden. Serve hot or cold.

Serves 6

pork with orange and cranberry

ingredients

> 1 cup orange juice
> 2 teaspoons grated orange rind
> 1/4 teaspoon ground cloves

> 3 tablespoons cranberry sauce
> 4 butterfly pork steaks, trimmed of fat
> cracked black pepper
> 1 tablespoon oil

method

1. Combine orange juice, orange rind, cloves and cranberry sauce in a glass bowl. Add pork and marinate for 1-2 hours.

2. Drain pork and coat with black pepper. Heat oil in a nonstick frying pan. Cook pork for 4-5 minutes each side or to your liking. Keep warm.

3. Strain marinade into pan. Bring to the boil and reduce slightly. Spoon over pork and serve.

Serves 4

grilled lamb cutlets

ingredients

> 8 lamb cutlets, trimmed of fat
> 1 teaspoon fresh

> oregano leaves
> freshly ground black pepper
> 2 tablespoons olive oil

method

1. Place cutlets on a plate. Season with oregano and black pepper to taste, brush with oil and marinate for 30 minutes.
2. Cook cutlets under a preheated medium grill for 3-4 minutes each side or to your liking. Serve immediately.

Serves 4

red currant lamb

ingredients

> 4 large lamb chops, trimmed of fat
> freshly ground black

> pepper
> 1 tablespoon lime juice
> 1/2 cup red currant jelly
> 2 tablespoons mustard

method

1. Season chops with black pepper to taste. Grill for 4-5 minutes each side or until cooked to your liking. Keep warm.
2. Place lime juice, red currant jelly and mustard in a small saucepan and cook gently until jelly melts and sauce is smooth. Spoon over chops and serve.

Serves 4

marinated steaks

ingredients

> 1 teaspoon curry powder
> 2 tablespoons brown sugar
> 2 tablespoons tomato sauce

> 2 teaspoons Worcestershire sauce
> 1 teaspoon soy sauce
> 2 teaspoons lime juice
> 4 rib-eye steaks, trimmed of fat

method

1. Combine curry powder, sugar, tomato sauce, Worcestershire sauce, soy sauce and lime juice in a glass bowl. Add meat and marinate for 2-4 hours.
2. Drain meat and cook on a preheated medium-high barbecue, basting frequently with marinade, for 3-4 minutes each side or to your liking.

Serves 4

bean and sausage cobbler

ingredients

> 1 tablespoon oil
> 1 onion, chopped
> 6 pork or beef sausages
> 14 oz/440 g canned tomatoes, undrained and mashed
> 10 oz/315 g canned red kidney beans, rinsed

> 8 oz/250 g broccoli flowerets
> 1 green pepper, chopped
> $1/2$ teaspoon chili powder
> 11 oz/350 g packet scone mix
> 4 oz/125 g grated mature Cheddar cheese

method

1. Heat oil in a frying pan over medium heat and cook

onion, stirring, for 3 minutes or until soft. Add
sausages and cook, turning several times,
for 10 minutes or until brown on all sides.

2. Slice sausages lengthwise and place in a casserole
with onion. Stir in tomatoes, beans, broccoli, green
pepper and chili powder, cover and bake at
375°F/190°C/Gas 5 for 30 minutes.

3. Make up scone mix according to packet directions.
Roll out dough and cut out rounds. Place rounds on
top of sausage mixture, sprinkle with cheese and bake
for 30 minutes longer or until topping is cooked and
cheese melts.

Serves 4

fluffy chocolate mousse

ingredients

> 2 oz/60 g butter
> 3$^1/_2$ oz/100 g dark chocolate
> 1 teaspoon orange rind
> 1 tablespoon coffee liqueur (optional)
> 3 eggs, separated
> $^1/_4$ cup warm water
> 3 tablespoons sugar
> 2 tablespoons cream, whipped

method

1. Melt butter and chocolate in a bowl over simmering water, stirring constantly. Cool to room temperature. Stir in orange rind and liqueur (if using).

2. Beat egg yolks and water with an electric mixer until light and fluffy, about 5 minutes. Fold into chocolate mixture until combined.

3. Beat egg whites with sugar until stiff peaks form. Fold into chocolate mixture. Pour into serving glasses and refrigerate for 2 hours. Decorate with cream.

Serves 4

apple pudding

ingredients

> **6 green apples, cored, peeled and sliced**
> **3^1/2 oz/100 g raisins**
> **2 oz/60 g pine nuts, toasted**
> **1 cup orange juice**
> **^{1}/4 cup honey**
> **2 oz/60 g ground almonds**
> **1 tablespoon grated orange rind**
> **6 whole cloves**
> **^{1}/2 teaspoon ground cinnamon**

method

1. Layer apples, raisins and pine nuts in a shallow ovenproof dish. Pour over orange juice, drizzle with honey and sprinkle with almonds, orange rind, cloves and cinnamon.
2. Cover dish with aluminum foil and bake at 400°F/200°C/ Gas 6 for 35-40 minutes or until apples are tender.

Serves 4

queen of puddings

ingredients

> **2 cups milk, scalded**
> **3 eggs, separated**
> **1 teaspoon vanilla extract**

> **3 tablespoons sugar**
> **6 slices white bread, crusts removed, cubed**
> **3 tablespoons raspberry jam**

method

1. Beat hot milk, egg yolks, vanilla and 1 tablespoon sugar until combined. Stir in bread cubes. Pour mixture into a lightly greased ovenproof dish. Place in a baking dish filled halfway up with water and bake at 350°F/180°C/Gas 4 for 45 minutes.

2. Beat egg whites until stiff peaks form, then fold in remaining sugar. Spread jam over pudding and top with meringue. If liked, decorate by dropping small teaspoons of extra jam on top of meringue. Bake for 15 minutes longer or until meringue is golden and crisp. Serve warm or at room temperature.

Serves 6

lemon parfaits

ingredients

> **1 tablespoon grated lemon rind**
> **$1/2$ cup lemon juice**
> **3 large eggs, separated**
> **$5^{1}/2$ oz/170 g sugar**
> **1 cup heavy cream, stiffly whipped**

method

1. Combine lemon rind, lemon juice, egg yolks and half the sugar in a small enameled saucepan. Beat well, then place over low heat and stir until thick, without boiling. Cool.

2. Beat egg whites until soft peaks form, gradually add remaining sugar and continue beating until stiff peaks form.
3. Fold meringue and whipped cream into lemon mixture. Spoon into glasses and chill until ready to serve. Decorate with shredded lemon rind and sugared violets if desired.

Serves 6

rum balls

ingredients

> **2 cups plain chocolate cake crumbs**
> **2 tablespoons powdered sugar**
> **2 tablespoons cocoa powder**
> **6 1/2 oz/200 g dark chocolate, melted**
> **1/4 cup heavy cream**
> **2 tablespoons rum**

> **6 1/2 oz/200 g dark chocolate, melted, extra**

method

1. Blend or process cake crumbs with powdered sugar, cocoa powder, chocolate, cream and rum until quite smooth. Transfer to a large bowl, cover and refrigerate until firm.
2. Shape mixture into balls. Dip in extra chocolate and place on a foil-lined tray. Decorate each ball with a small piece of sugared violet if desired. Allow to set, then chill until ready to serve.

Makes about 30

basic scones

ingredients
- 8 oz/250 g self-raising flour
- 1 teaspoon baking powder
- 2 teaspoons sugar
- $1\frac{1}{2}$ oz/45 g butter, chopped
- 1 egg, lightly beaten
- $\frac{1}{2}$ cup milk

method
1. Sift flour and baking powder together into a bowl, add sugar. Rub in butter, using fingertips, until mixture resembles breadcrumbs. Using a fork, mix egg and most of the milk into flour mixture, adding remaining milk if necessary to make a soft dough.
2. Knead with fingertips on a lightly floured surface until smooth. Using heel of hand, press dough out to $\frac{3}{4}$ in/2 cm thickness. Cut scones out with a floured 2 in/5 cm cutter. Arrange on a greased and lightly floured baking tray. Brush with milk and bake at 440ºF/ 220°C/ Gas 7 for 15-20 minutes or until golden.

Makes 10

fruity wholewheat rolls

ingredients

> **2 cups wholewheat flour**
> **2 cups self-raising flour**
> **1/2 teaspoon ground nutmeg**
> **1/2 teaspoon ground cinnamon**
> **1 cup dried mixed fruits**
> **1 1/2 cups buttermilk**

method

1. Sift together flours, nutmeg and cinnamon into a bowl. Mix in dried fruits. Stir in buttermilk a little at a time and beat until dough is firm and leaves the side of the bowl.

2. Knead briefly on a lightly floured surface. Shape into 8 rolls. Place on a lightly greased baking tray and, using a sharp knife, score the top into 8 segments. Bake at 400°F/200°C/Gas 6 for 30-35 minutes or until well risen and golden.

Serves 8

yogurt cheesecake

ingredients

- > 4 oz/125 g plain sweet cookies, crushed
- > 2 oz/60 g butter, melted
- > 1 lb/500 g cream cheese, softened
- > 1 cup yogurt of your choice
- > 3 eggs
- > 1/2 cup heavy cream
- > 3 1/2 oz/100 g sugar
- > 3 teaspoons finely grated lemon rind

method

1. Combine cookies and butter in a bowl. Press mixture over the base of a well greased springform pan and refrigerate until firm.

2. Beat cream cheese in a bowl until smooth. Add yogurt, eggs, cream, sugar and lemon rind and beat to combine.

3. Pour cream cheese mixture into prepared pan and bake at 300ºF/150ºC/Gas 2 for 1 hour or until firm. Cool cheesecake in pan to room temperature, then chill until ready to serve.

Serves 8